The Psalms of David

24 Psalms for the Church's Year

Heinrich Schütz (1585–1672)

English adaptation by Albert and Marian Blackwell

MUSIC DEPARTMENT

OXFORD

UNIVERSITY PRESS

OXFORD
UNIVERSITY PRESS

198 Madison Avenue, New York, NY 10016, USA
Great Clarendon Street, Oxford OX2 6DP, England

Oxford University Press is a department of the University of Oxford.
It furthers the University's aim of excellence in research, scholarship,
and education by publishing worldwide

Oxford New York
Auckland Bangkok Buenos Aires Cape Town Chennai
Dar es Salaam Delhi Hong Kong Istanbul Karachi Kolkata
Kuala Lumpur Madrid Melbourne Mexico City Mumbai Nairobi
São Paulo Shanghai Taipei Tokyo Toronto

Oxford is a registered trademark of Oxford University Press

1 3 5 7 9 10 8 6 4 2

ISBN 978–0–19–386951–6

Music and text origination by
Barnes Music Engraving Ltd, East Sussex, England
Printed by Halstan & Co Ltd., England, on acid-free paper.

Contents

Introduction

Thy statutes have been my songs in the house of my pilgrimage.
Psalm 119: 54

Historical notes

In 1602 a Leipzig theologian, Cornelius Becker, published a German version of the Psalms. Becker paraphrased the Psalms freely in strophic, rhymed verses which congregations could sing to familiar hymn tunes. In 1628 Heinrich Schütz published musical settings of one hundred and two of Becker's Psalm texts under a full-page title beginning *Psalmen Davids* .... For twelve of his melodies Schütz used familiar tunes. He composed afresh the remaining melodies and all of the harmonizations.

Schütz's dedication of the *Psalmen Davids* offers a touching glimpse into his personal circumstances. In 1625 untimely death had taken his beloved wife of six years. Following the "lamentable loss of my dear, late wife Magdalene Wildeck," Schütz writes, work on "this little book of Psalms" has been "solace for my sorrow" and "a comforter in my sadness."

Schütz wrote these Psalm settings for observance of the Daily Office in his own household. Later, they were sung by the chapel choir of the Dresden court, where Schütz was *Kapellmeister*. Upon publication, the *Psalmen Davids* quickly enjoyed wider appeal, becoming Schütz's only compositions to appear in several editions during his lifetime. They were reissued unaltered in 1640. In 1661 Schütz published a revised edition, enlarged to include all one hundred and fifty of Becker's Psalms.

One of the defining marks of Schütz's musical genius is his sensitivity to texts. The aim in this edition has been to match English lyrics to Schütz's music as well as Schütz matched his music to Becker's German. To this end, the English lyrics exactly duplicate the German meter, syllable placement, and rhyme scheme.

The lyrics of this edition are not otherwise based on Becker's paraphrases, however, which take excessive liberties with the biblical Psalms. Rather, these lyrics follow standard English translations, with the Hebrew text as a touchstone. Their diction echoes the King James Version of the Bible, which appeared in 1611, about midway between Becker's 1602 paraphrases and Schütz's musical settings of 1628.

The musical transcriptions are based on *Heinrich Schütz: Neue Ausgabe sämtlicher Werke*, Vol. 6, edited by Walter Blankenburg (Bärenreiter, 1957), used by permission. Most are from Schütz's revised edition of 1661, but Psalms 84, 121, and 150 are from the first edition of 1628, where rhythms are more vigorous and the part writing more adventuresome.

The selection of twenty-four Psalms for this collection is based on frequency of occurrence in church lectionaries and association with the holy days of Christmas, The Holy Name, The Epiphany, The Presentation, The Annunciation, Palm Sunday, Easter, Ascension, The Visitation, Pentecost, Trinity Sunday, The Transfiguration, Holy Cross, and All Saints.

Performance notes

Schütz presents the Psalms in straightforward four-part settings, yet their angular melodies, exploring harmonies, and shifting rhythms have proved a little complex for congregational use. As a result, few of Schütz's settings have appeared in hymnals—in contrast, for example, with those of his sixteenth-century predecessors Claude Goudimel and Louis Bourgeois. An exception is No. 452 in *The Hymnal 1982* of the Episcopal Church, where Schütz's musical setting for Psalm 47 is paired with a twentieth-century lyric by F. Pratt Green, "Glorious the day when Christ was born."

For choirs and choruses, however, these miniature masterpieces are wonderfully accessible. Ensembles of all sizes and degrees of ability can enjoy them, singing in parts or in unison, *a cappella* or to the accompaniment of organ, winds, or strings.

Schütz's melodies are vocal delights. His harmonies can surprise us, but upon repetition they quickly seem inevitable. Likewise with his rhythms, which soon have singers humming and drumming their duple-triple alternations long after rehearsal is over. A good approach to mastering Schütz's metrical patterns is first to have singers speak the lyric in rhythm, thinking of entire phrases of text as single units, and noting how the words give logic to the rhythmic variations.

Each Psalm may be thought of as a dance—joyous, reflective, or somber in mood, but always patterned and pulsing. Final unstressed syllables should be greatly lightened, as in the words "dwelling" and "swelling" in Psalm 84, "thanksgiving" and "everliving" in Psalm 111, and the like. In contrast, Schütz offers us moments of great rhythmic vigor, as in the final bar of Psalm 98 and the "Hallelujah's" that conclude Psalm 47.

In his Preface to the *Psalmen Davids* Schütz recommends tempos that present the texts with "liveliness" yet without taking away from their proper "gravity." This edition's markings are merely suggestions of how Schütz's description might translate into metronome settings.

ALBERT BLACKWELL

to John R. Ferris, University Organist and Choirmaster,
The Memorial Church, Harvard University, 1958–90

Psalm 1

(Verses 1–3)

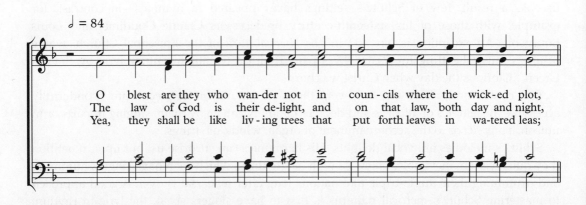

O blest are they who wan-der not in coun-cils where the wick-ed plot,
The law of God is their de-light, and on that law, both day and night,
Yea, they shall be like liv-ing trees that put forth leaves in wa-tered leas;

nor lin-ger in the sin-ners' way, nor with the scorn-ful go a-stray.
these bles-sed ones will me-di-tate: its Au-thor know-eth well their state.
and what-so-ev-er their pur-suit shall with God's bless-ing bring forth fruit.

OXFORD UNIVERSITY PRESS, 198 MADISON AVENUE, NEW YORK, NY 10016

Psalm 8

(Verses 1–8)

♩ = 78

O God, who art our Sov'-reign, ex - alt-ed is thy Name;
When I sur-vey cre - a - tion, the work of thine own hand,
Yet thou hast crowned with glo - ry the child-ren of thy hands,

the mouths of babes and child - ren thy ma - je - sty pro - claim.
the spheres in their ro - ta - tion, whose course thou hast or - dained:
and set them lit - tle low - er than thy an - gel - ic bands.

A - bove the heav - en's height, from ho - ly sanc - tu - a - ry,
Why dost thou care for man, that for his weal thou mind - est,
Do - min - ion thou hast giv'n, to tend with due de - vo - tion,

to quell the ad - ver - sa - ry, thou show - est forth thy might.
be - stow - est lov - ing kind - ness? What is this son of man?
in earth and sky and o - cean, all crea - tures un - der heav'n.

Psalm 16

(Verses 1–3, 5–6, 9–11)

God keep me, for I trust in thee: to God my soul hath spo - ken;
Our God is mine in - he - ri-tance, and is my cup and por - tion;
My flesh shall al - so rest in hope, for thou wilt not sur - ren - der

Thou art my God, and next to thine, my good - ness is but to - ken.
mine eyes sur - vey a plea - sant land, God's lov - ing care my for - tune.
my soul up - on death's dark'-ning slope: thou art my strong de - fend - er.

Thy ho - ly peo - ple in the land,
I'll bless our God who guid - eth me,
Thou sav - est me from mor - tal strife,

the   no - ble   saints   in   thy   right   hand:
whose   gra - cious hand   pro - vi - deth   me:
and   show - est   me   the   path   of   life,

in   them   I   find   my   plea - sure.
my   heart   there - fore   re - joic - eth.
where plea - sures are   for - ev - er.

Psalm 23

(Verses 1–6)

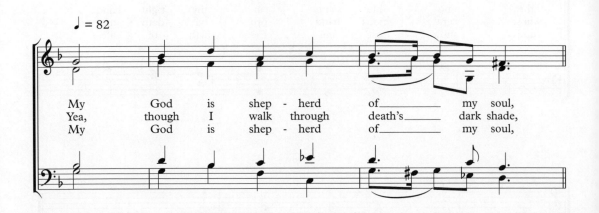

My God is shep - herd of_____ my soul,
Yea, though I walk through death's_____ dark shade,
My God is shep - herd of_____ my soul,

my ev - 'ry want sup - ply - ing,
no e - vil shall dis - turb_____ me;
my ev - 'ry want sup - ply - ing,

sus - tain - ing_____ me by wa - ters still
thy pro - vi - dence shall be_____ my aid,
sus - tain - ing_____ me by wa - ters still

Psalm 33

(Verses 1–5, 12–22)

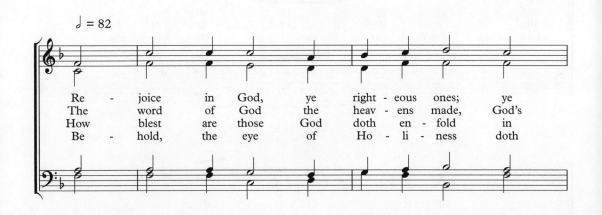

Re - joice in God, ye right - eous ones; ye
The word of God the heav - ens made, God's
How blest are those God doth en - fold in
Be - hold, the eye of Ho - li - ness doth

just, now join in prais - ing; your skill with harp and
breath, the heav'n - ly or - der, the depth of o - cean
arms of sure sal - va - tion, whose right - eous gaze earth
all the earth ex - a - mine to pluck our lives from

horns of bronze due praise to God up - rais - ing.
wa - ters laid, held in by coast - land bor - der.
doth be - hold and form - eth ev' - ry na - tion.
jaws of death and feed in time of fa - mine.

Sing forth new songs to God a - bove,
Let all the earth then stand in____ awe,
God com - pre - hend - eth ev' - ry____ deed:
Our souls a - wait our Help - er____ just,

who fill - eth earth with truth and love,
and na - tions fear God's stead - fast law,
we are not saved by strength or steed,
whose ho - ly Name in - vit - eth trust.

with right - eous - ness and____ jus - tice.
whose will a - bid - eth____ ev - er.
but by our ho - ly____ Ma - ker.
God's mer - cy be up - on us!

Psalm 40

(Verses 1–11)

♩ = 62

I waited for my Savior, who stooped and heard my cry;
How blessed they who trust thee, and from all idols turn.
I love to do thy bidding; thy law is deep within.

from pit of mire my Helper secured my feet on high.
Thou hast done great things for me; with thee compareth none.
I tell thy righteous tidings; nought doth my lips restrain.

Now in my mouth a new song proclaimeth praise of God,
How vast thy plans and wonders: O might I make them known!
All this, my God, thou knowest: thy love do not withhold.

declareth awe the day long, and spreadeth truth abroad.
Yea, far exceed our numbers the marvels thou hast done.
Compassion thou bestowest; let it my soul enfold.

Psalm 47

(Verses 1–2, 5–9)

O clap your hands, ye peo - ple all, and shout to God your rous - ing call;
Our God as - cend - eth with a shout; tri - um - phant trum - pet tones ring out.
God rul - eth earth with heav'n - ly will; to songs of praise ap - ply your skill.

for God most high in - spir - eth fear, who rul - eth, earth's great O - ver - seer.
Sing prais - es to our God on high; with joy let praise to praise re - ply.
Ex - alt - ed far a - bove the sky, God's Ho - li - ness doth reign on high.

Hal - le - lu - jah! Hal - le - lu - jah! Hal - le - lu - jah!
Hal - le - lu - jah! Hal - le - lu - jah! Hal - le - lu - jah!
Hal - le - lu - jah! Hal - le - lu - jah! Hal - le - lu - jah!

Psalm 66

(Verses 1–2, 5–6, 8–9)

Psalm 72

(Verses 1–4, 10–17)

Psalm 84

(Verses 1–3, 10–12)

♩. = 54

How love - ly is thy dwell-ing, O God of hosts_ to me,
Be - hold, the spar - row find - eth an house where-in___ to rest;
A thou - sand days com - pare not to one day in___ thy courts.

my heart with ar - dor swell-ing thy courts once more_ to see.
the swal - low al - so mind-eth her fledg - ling in___ the nest.
The tents of e - vil snare not the keep - er of___ thy doors,

For them my spir - it long-eth; my faint-ing heart be - long-eth,
E'en thine own al - tars ho - ly shel-ter thy crea - tures low - ly,
where glo - ry shin - eth bright-ly on all who walk up - right-ly,

O liv - ing God,_____ to thee.
safe in thy courts,_____ most blest.
trust - ing thee e - - - - ver - more.

Psalm 96

(Verses 1–4, 9–13)

Psalm 98

(Verses 1–9)

Psalm 99

(Verses 1–9)

Psalm 100

(Verses 1–5)

Psalm 104

(Verses 24–31, 33, 35)

God, how ma - ni - fold thy world; sun and moon and stars un - furled,
All thy crea - tures look to thee for their food in due de - gree.
Then thy Spir - it com - eth fresh and earth's face re - ceiv - eth breath.

liv - ing things, both great and small: ho - ly Wis - dom made them all.
Thou pro - vid - est what they need, thy hand giv - eth and they feed;
May God's glo - ry shine for aye, grate - ful earth re - new al - way.

Yon - der is the bound-less sea, teem - ing with fe - cun - di - ty,
thy face hid - eth and they quake, life and breath their souls for - sake,
Ev - er to my God I'll sing, bless - ings to my Ma - ker bring,

crea - tures sport - ing, glad_____ and free.
death and dust their lives_____ o'er - take.
let my Hal - le - lu - jah ring.

Psalm 111

(Verses 1–10)

♩ = 80

Heart, soul, and strength, I of - fer God thanks-giv - ing,
God giv - eth food to all who live in rev' - rence,
God through the cho - sen peo - ple is re - deem - ing

in as - sem - bly with the up - right.
all who trust the care of God's hand.
all who live in awe of God's Name,

Great are God's deeds of mer - cy ev - er - liv - ing,
They know God's stead - fast love and gra - cious pres - ence,
ev - er the ho - ly cov - e - nant es - teem - ing,

bring - ing faith - ful peo-ple de - light. *Ky - ri - e - lei - son.*
grant - ing fruit - ful gifts of the land. *Ky - ri - e - lei - son.*
through all a - ges e - ver the same. *Ky - ri - e - lei - son.*

Pow'r and splen - dor grace God's ho - ly Name,
Ho - ly truth____ and grace are ev - er sure.
Fear of God____ be - gin - neth wis - dom true.

ma - jes - ty from age to age the same, won-drous works from a - bove
Just com - mand - ments al - ways shall en - dure, stand - ing fast, ev - er true,
Bles - sed they whom Wis-dom doth en - due. Right-eous deeds all our days

man - i - fest - ing heav'n - ly love. Ky - ri - e - lei - son.
grant - ing life and mak - ing new. Ky - ri - e - lei - son.
ren - der God our fit - ting praise. Ky - ri - e - lei - son.

Psalm 113

(Verses 1–9)

♩. = 54

Hal - le - lu - jah! Sing prais - es, ye faith - ful ser - vants of___ our God.
Who like our God ex - cell - eth, yet stoop - eth heav'n and earth_ to see,

Hal - le - lu - jah! Your voic - es now join, the sa - cred Name to laud.
and with the need - y dwell - eth, from dust and ash - es to___ set free?

O let that Name be bles - sed, from this_____ time e - ver - more,___
Who set - eth them with prin - ces that dwell_____ in high a - bode,___

God's ho - ly Name pro - fess - ed, ex - tolled from shore to shore.___
and child - less wo - men send - eth the joy of mo - ther - hood.___

From ris - ing sun to set - ting the Name of God be praised,___
Hal - le - lu - jah! Sing prais - es, ye ser - vants of our God.___

God's glo - ry high be - fit - ting, all hands to heav'n up - raised,___
Hal - le - lu - jah! Your voi - ces now join, God's Name to laud,___

all hands to heaven up - raised.
now join, God's Name to laud.

Psalm 118

(Verses 14–17, 19–23, 25–6, 28–9)

♩ = 70

Our God is my sal - va - tion, my strength and joy - ful song.
Fling wide the right - eous por - tals and I will en - ter in
Ho - san - nah, glad Ho - san - nah! God send us now suc - cess.

The sounds of ex - ul - ta - tion in right - eous tents be - long.
a - mong the thank - ful mor - tals de - li - vered from their sin.
Ho - san - nah, glad Ho - san - nah! Hail him our God doth bless.

My God's right hand doth give_____ most right - eous vin - di - ca - tion
The once re - ject - ed stone,_____ the work of God's own do - ing,
Give thanks, for God is good,_____ whose mer - cy fail - eth nev - er,

and   ho - ly   ac - cla - ma - tion. I   shall not die, but   live,_____
our   lives from death re - new - ing, is   now the cor - ner - stone,_____
whose love en - dur - eth ev - er, at   all times firm - ly   stood,_____

I   shall   not   die,   but   live.
is   now   the   cor - ner - stone.
at   all   times firm - ly   stood.

Psalm 119

(Verses 1–16)

♩ = 70

How bles - sed are the blame - less who prac - tice what is right,
O may my ways be guid - ed to keep thy ho - ly laws,
By keep - ing thy com - mand - ments the young may cleanse their way.
My lips, in all their speak - ing, thy judg - ments will re - cite.

do ser - vice with the guilt - less, seek God with their whole might.
that I might not be chid - ed when du - ty ov - er - awes.
My heart pur - sues thy judg - ments; O let my path not stray.
While o - thers wealth are seek - ing, in thee I take de - light.

Thou didst thy ho - ly laws re - veal, and thou hast us com - mand - ed
Un - feign - ed thanks I of - fer thee, and pray that thou might ne - ver
I guard thy pro - mise in my heart, that I might keep thy sta - tutes.
My mind e'er holds thy word in awe, and in my me - di - ta - tions

to keep them all with zeal.
with - hold thy grace from me.
How bles - sed God, thou art.
will ne'er for - get thy law.

Psalm 121

(Verses 1–8)

28

Psalm 122

(Verses 1–9)

Glad was my heart when my ears heard, "Let us God's dwell - ing en - ter."
Whith - er the tribes of Is - ra - el, God-fear-ing tribes___ as - sem - bling,
Pray peace with - in Je - ru - sa - lem: may they who love___ thee pros - per;

And now our feet, led by this word, stand in thy gates,___ O Tem - ple.
the ho - ly Name glad - ly forth tell, prais-ing in fear___ and trem - bling.
may qui - et - ness and peace des-cend on ev' - ry wall___ and tow - er.

Je - ru - sa - lem:___ ci - ty of God, built on a hill,___ sa - cred a - bode
For there the thrones__ of jus-tice shine, the thrones of Da - vid's roy - al line,
For all thy chil - dren thus I pray, and for thy ho - ly Tem-ple say:

of peace and jus - tice hal - lowed.
dis - pens - ing judg - ment ho - ly.
"May good be thine___ for - ev - er."

Psalm 126

(Verses 1–6)

30

Psalm 149

(Verses 1–5)

♩ = 84

O sing to God a new song, sing praise, sing Hal - le - lu;
Let strings of harp re - sound - ing new songs of praise_____ com - pose.

a - midst the con - gre - ga - tion, sing faith - ful saints_____ and true.
God's ho - ly grace a - bound - ing grants stead - fast saints_____ re - pose.

Sing praise to Is - rael's Glo - ry, re - joice on Zi - on's height.
From beds of joy and tri - umph, ye faith - ful saints and true,

Ex - ult, ye poor and low - ly, in whom is God's_____ de - light.
O sing to God a new_____ song, sing praise, sing Hal - le - lu!

Psalm 150

(Verses 1–6)

Hal - le - lu - jah! praise God on high, Hal - le - lu - jah! and glo - ri - fy,
Hal - le - lu - jah! let trum - pets sound, Hal - le - lu - jah! and harps re - sound,
Hal - le - lu - jah! now drum and string, Hal - le - lu - jah! and voi - ces ring.

Hal - le - lu - jah! the First and Last, Hal - le - lu - jah! for great - ness vast.
Hal - le - lu - jah! the cym - bals loud, Hal - le - lu - jah! and tim - brels proud.
Let the re - sound - ing or - ches - tra praise with one breath: Hal - le - lu - jah!

Liturgical Index

Seasons	Particularly appropriate psalms
Advent	72, 122, 126
Christmas	84, 96, 98
Epiphany	1, 40, 96, 99, 111, 113, 119
Lent	16, 23, 33, 119, 121, 122, 126
Easter	1, 8, 16, 23, 33, 47, 66, 98, 100, 111, 118, 150

Holy Days	
The Holy Name (January 1)	8
The Epiphany (January 6)	72
The Presentation (February 2)	84
The Annunciation (March 25)	40
Palm Sunday	118
Ascension	47
The Visitation (May 31)	113
Pentecost	33, 100, 104
Trinity Sunday	8, 33, 150
The Transfiguration (August 6)	99
Holy Cross (September 14)	40, 98
All Saints	149

Lectionary Occurrences
of Psalms in this Collection

BCP = *The Book of Common Prayer* (Episcopal)
LFM = *Lectionary for Mass* (Roman Catholic)
RCL = *The Revised Common Lectionary* (Ecumenical)

Psalm 1
    BCP: Epiphany 6 C; Proper 1 C; Proper 18 C; Proper 25 C; St. James of Jerusalem;
        Of a Saint III; At Confirmation
    LFM: 6th Ordinary C
    RCL: Epiphany 6 C; Easter 7 B; Proper 18 C; Proper 20 B; Proper 25 A

Psalm 8
    BCP: Proper 22 B; Holy Name ABC; Easter Thursday ABC; Vocation in Daily Work
    LFM: Easter Thursday ABC; Trinity Sunday C
    RCL: Holy Name ABC; Trinity Sunday AC; New Year ABC; Proper 22 B

Psalm 16
    BCP: Lent 2 B; Easter Vigil ABC; Easter Monday ABC; Proper 8 C; Proper 28 B;
        For All Baptized Christians
    LFM: Easter Vigil ABC; Easter Monday ABC; Easter 3 A; 13th Ordinary C; 33rd Ordinary B
    RCL: Easter Vigil ABC; Easter 2 A; Proper 8 C; Proper 28 B

Psalm 23
    BCP: Lent 4 A; Easter 4 AB; Proper 23 A; Confession of St. Peter; At Baptism; At a Burial
    LFM: Lent 4 A; Easter 4 A; 16th Ordinary B; 28th Ordinary A; Last Ordinary (Christ the
        King) A; Sacred Heart C
    RCL: Lent 4 A; Easter 4 ABC; Proper 11 B; Proper 23 A

Psalm 33
    BCP: Lent 2 A; Easter Vigil ABC; Easter Tuesday ABC; Easter 3 C; Easter 5 A; Easter 6 B;
        Pentecost ABC; Proper 14 C
    LFM: Lent 2 A; Easter Vigil ABC; Easter Thursday ABC; Easter 5 A; Trinity Sunday B;
        19th Ordinary C; 29th Ordinary B
    RCL: Proper 5 A; Proper 14 C

Psalm 40
    BCP: Good Friday ABC; Epiphany 2 A; Annunciation ABC; Holy Cross ABC
    LFM: 2nd Ordinary AB; 20th Ordinary C; Annunciation
    RCL: Epiphany 2 A; Annunciation ABC

Psalm 47
    BCP: Easter 7 ABC; Ascension ABC; For the Nation
    LFM: Ascension C
    RCL: Ascension ABC

Psalm 66
> **BCP**: Easter 5 AB; Proper 9 C
> **LFM**: Easter 6 A; 14th Ordinary C
> **RCL**: Easter 6 A; Proper 9 C; Proper 23 C

Psalm 72
> **BCP**: Advent 2 A; Epiphany ABC; For Social Service
> **LFM**: Advent 2 A; Epiphany ABC
> **RCL**: Advent 2 A; Epiphany ABC

Psalm 84
> **BCP**: Christmas 2 ABC; The Presentation; Proper 25 C; At Baptism; Of a Pastor II; Ordination of a Deacon; Consecration of a Church; Anniversary of the Dedication of a Church
> **LFM**: Christmas 1 C
> **RCL**: Presentation ABC; Proper 16 B; Proper 25 C

Psalm 96
> **BCP**: Christmas Day I ABC; Epiphany 2 C; Proper 4 C; Proper 24 A; Of a Missionary I; For the Mission of the Church
> **LFM**: Christmas (Midnight) ABC; 2nd Ordinary C; 29th Ordinary A
> **RCL**: Christmas Day I ABC; Epiphany 9 C; Proper 4 C; Proper 24 A

Psalm 98
> **BCP**: Christmas Day III ABC; Easter Vigil ABC; Easter 3 B; Proper 28 C; Holy Cross ABC; Of a Missionary II
> **LFM**: Christmas Day ABC; Easter 6 B; 28th Ordinary C; 33rd Ordinary C; The Immaculate Conception ABC
> **RCL**: Christmas Day III ABC; Easter Vigil ABC; Easter 6 B; Proper 27 C; Proper 28 C; Holy Cross ABC

Psalm 99
> **BCP**: Last Sunday after Epiphany AC; Transfiguration ABC; For the Ministry I; Ordination of a Bishop
> **LFM**: —
> **RCL**: Last Epiphany (Transfiguration) AC; Proper 24 A

Psalm 100
> **BCP**: Proper 4 BC; Proper 6 A; Ordination of a Bishop
> **LFM**: Easter 4 C; 11th Ordinary A
> **RCL**: Proper 6 A; Last of Pentecost (Reign of Christ) A; Thanksgiving C

Psalm 104
> **BCP**: Pentecost ABC; For Rogation Days III
> **LFM**: Easter Vigil ABC; Pentecost Vigil ABC; Pentecost ABC; 1st Ordinary C
> **RCL**: Pentecost ABC; Proper 24 B

Psalm 111
    BCP: Epiphany 4 B; Easter 2 ABC; Of the Incarnation
    LFM: —
    RCL: Epiphany 4 B; Proper 15 B; Proper 23 C

Psalm 113
    BCP: Epiphany 3 C; Proper 23 C; The Visitation
    LFM: 25th Ordinary C
    RCL: Visitation ABC; Proper 20 C

Psalm 118
    BCP: Palm Sunday ABC; Easter Day ABC; Daily in Easter Week ABC; Easter 2 ABC
    LFM: Easter Vigil ABC; Easter Day ABC; Easter Friday ABC; Easter Saturday ABC;
            Easter 2 ABC; Easter 4 B
    RCL: Palm Sunday ABC; Easter ABC; Easter 2 C

Psalm 119
    BCP: Epiphany 6 A; Proper 1 A; Proper 26 B
    LFM: 6th Ordinary A; 17th Ordinary A
    RCL: Epiphany 6 A; Lent 5 B; Proper 26 B

Psalm 121
    BCP: Proper 24 C; Of a Martyr I; At a Burial
    LFM: 29th Ordinary C
    RCL: Lent 2 A; Proper 24 C

Psalm 122
    BCP: Advent 1 A; Lent 4 B; Easter Vigil ABC; For the Unity of the Church
    LFM: Advent 1 A; Last Ordinary (Christ the King) C
    RCL: Advent 1 A

Psalm 126
    BCP: Advent 2 C; Advent 3 B; Lent 5 C; St. Thomas; Of a Martyr
    LFM: Advent 2 C; Lent 5 C; 30th Ordinary B
    RCL: Advent 3 B; Lent 5 C; Proper 25 B; Thanksgiving B

Psalm 149
    BCP: All Saints ABC
    LFM: —
    RCL: Proper 18 A; All Saints C

Psalm 150
    BCP: Trinity Sunday A
    LFM: —
    RCL: Easter 2 C